HOW TO MAKE MONEY ONLINE

ANTHONY EKANEM

ISBN 979-888521649-4

Contents

Preface

Everyone wants to make money. That's a given. And the internet can present some lucrative possibilities. But it can also create a breeding ground for scammers. Sometimes it's tough to know what a scam is and what isn't. No one can tell you in all honesty that they haven't, at some time in their online career, been taken at least once by a hyped-up scam. You must understand that there are some folks who are a constant source of helpful information, and those that are hanging out looking for quick cash.

While you can make some easy profits doing business on the internet, you still must be vigilant and careful when buying. The adage still rings true, especially online: "Let the Buyer Beware". Plus, when you sell products online, generally start-up costs are much lower than that of a traditional "brick-and-mortar" store. In many cases, your monthly costs would be less than going for a night out. So, turning a profit is much, much easier to accomplish.

Setting Your Hours

Who doesn't want to be their own boss? Deciding when and if you work gives you such a sense of freedom. Well, not exactly. A common misconception about a home-based business is that you will have much more time to do the things you want to, and less time spent working. You see it all the time if you've seen any type of "infomercial" when you're up late watching television. The fact of the matter is any business is still a business. Meaning, you must work at it to taste success. Many times, when running your own "stay at home business", there are more work hours put in, and less time for all the fun things that you thought you'd be doing. This is not meant to be discouraging, just a reality check. So be prepared for this ahead of time.

Limitless Opportunity

Earning money online is virtually limitless. Every single day, millions log on in search of something. Whether it be information or a specific product. Shopping by internet is a time-saver. Collecting information online is a time-saver. Understand that most folks looking for information are prepared to pay for it. This is a fact. And absolutely anything that you can think up can be turned into an informative product. Remember, there are millions of internet visitors across the world searching for information. The only "limits" involved with selling online are those you set for yourself.

Add to that the fact that with information selling, you can resell the same "packet" of materials repeatedly to as many people who want it, and you have an unstoppable income force! However, it's important to remember that technology is an ever-expanding field. So, you will have to "change with the times" and be prepared to keep your information up to date. Change is a good thing.

Any "idea" can be cultivated into a product. Does it have to be a great idea? No. But, you do need to make sure that you are offering something that has value. You can't just go and copy down some free information, change some of the wording, and then expect to make a profit. It doesn't work that way. You must put forth the effort to get value from what you're creating. This way, if you value and believe in what you have made, then most likely others will too. Plus, eventually, you'll get caught and be labelled a "scammer". And that, my friend, is a reputation you do not want if you want to make your online business a success.

CHAPTER ONE

Where to Sell Your Products

The first thing you need to do is have a place to sell your products from. It doesn't matter what you're selling, but it does matter where you sell it from. Let me explain. When you plan to run an online business, treat it like one! You'll make much more money this way, believe me. Sure, you'll have some out-of-pocket expenses, but that's part of doing business. I cannot stress enough the importance of having your very own domain name and website space.

There's a big difference between a department store and a yard sale. Think of your business as a specialized department store and give it a place to "stand". If you try to do everything for free, your business will suffer for it in the long run. You need complete control over your business. After all, you are the boss and not just the manager. That's why you need to steer clear of free web hosting sites. Yes, they give you your own sub-domain and a limited amount of space, but more importantly, these hosts hinder your earning ability with permanent banner ad placement and file upload limitations.

Keeping everything as simple as possible will benefit you in the end and make your job a lot easier. Don't waste your time or energy. It's not worth it. So, do yourself a big favour and pay for good web hosting. Let me add this, many web hosts are steering away from allowing certain files to be hosted on their servers. This includes .zip, .mp3, .exe, and in some cases .pdf files. Not good for an information business. Most of these web hosts who ban these types of files are offering "shared" hosting. Shared hosting is simply multiple websites that share the same server. While this isn't a bad system, it still limits what you can do. But, if you are comfortable with that and have found a shared hosting plan that fits your specific needs at a good price, then go for it. But be sure to check their terms of service before you finalize your choice and pay.

Before you set up with a specific web host, you need a domain name. That is an easy enough task. Where you purchase your domain name is just as important as where you purchase your webspace hosting. A good company to go with for domain name purchasing is NameCheap. They've been around for a while, and they have top-notch customer service. Plus, their prices are affordable.

When selecting the right domain name, it's a good idea for you to add at least one descriptive word about your online business. Say for instance you want to sell soccer equipment, you might choose www.waytogoalsoccer.com, www.soccersupplier.com, or www.yoursoccersupplies.net, www.justsoccer.com, etc. The reason for adding a "keyword" in your domain is that when people use search engines, your site will come up more frequently. And that means more traffic, which means more sales.

Now, if you're just beginning and don't have the funds to purchase a domain name and website space, there is another way to begin if you are wishing to sell information products that can be automatically delivered by way of downloading. There is a site that does something unique. I know I said earlier that using a sub-domain isn't a good idea for serious online business. But using a system like TradeBit is the exception to this.

And the reason is quite simple

First, you can get a free 20 MB account, a sub-domain, web-based FTP file uploading, a built-in shopping cart, your affiliate programme, and integrated PayPal/eBay selling plus automated product delivery. This will cut down your workload substantially. Beyond that, they have extensive tutorials in both text and flash that help you "learn the ropes" when using their system.

Besides this, you can always use the redirect function when you purchase your domain name and have a small web hosting space. You won't need a whole bunch of space if you use TradeBit to host your product files. And they allow you to host all the files that shared hosting companies do not. Such as .mp3, .exe, .zip, images, and the like. Understand that any files you host you must have the right to sell them. But if you are a reseller, then this is not a problem.

There is no good reason why purchasing a domain name and webspace should cost you more than $30 realistically. And, if you need more file hosting space, TradeBit offers affordable solutions for this as well that you can upgrade to at any time. All in all, setting up your own online business should cost you no more than $100.

A few more things you will need before you begin are a merchant account, an eBay account if you are interested in selling there, an HTML editor for making changes to pre-designed sales kits or for creating a sales page, and an image editor for creating graphics for your sales pages and products.

There are several different places where you can pick up your merchant account. PayPal is a top choice because it's free. Plus, this is the payment system that TradeBit uses although they are working on adding other systems at the time of this writing. Now, for those that cannot get a PayPal account because of restrictions, you can always get a free merchant account from StormPay. It's basically the same system setup as PayPal. But you can sign up for a free merchant account on a new system called PayDotCom. They offer PayPal and StormPay integration among others within their system, so it's a good choice. Again, opening a merchant account with PayDotCom is free.

If you have the money and can afford it, there are other merchant account systems out there too. ClickBank is the first on my list. It will cost around $50 to set this up. But don't worry, it's just a one-time fee. Also, there is 2CheckOut and they offer a free shopping cart set up service.

CHAPTER TWO

What Products to Sell

1. Information Products

This type of selling is probably the easiest way to make fast money without huge overhead costs. And you also can sell unlimited amounts of information products to as many customers as you can sell them too. But you must make sure that the information products that you have in stock come with something called Master Resale Rights. Master Resale Rights makes it possible within the product terms to resell not only the product itself but also the right to resell it to those customers you sell it to.

While there are also Standard/Basic/Full Resale Rights, the definition of this is much different. These types of resalable products only give you, the original purchaser of the product to resell it, and not those you sell it to.

Even though Standard/Basic/Full Resale Rights is not a bad thing, having the Master Resale Rights will most certainly bring in more profits since your customers can also make money with them as well as learning something at the same time.

With that said, you need to be selective on which resale rights products you buy. What you need to be looking for is a product that is: (1) newer, and (2). unique. These criteria usually make for the best sellers. The reason for this is quite simple. Lots of people jump online searching for an opportunity that will make them some fast cash. The information product business excels in this capacity. That's why so many hop onto the resale rights information selling bandwagon. However, many fail at running a successful information e-business because they have no clue as to what they need to be selling! Or even how to go about selecting a killer product that will generate excellent profits for them without costing them an arm and a leg.

As I said before, you must be extremely picky. And be wary of "hyped" up sites. Just because the site says that the product is a #1, doesn't mean that it is. There are lots of stinkers out there. Remember that the owner of the website that is in essence "pushing" a specific product are in the same boat you are. They want to earn money. Things like "I'll be raising the price soon", "Time Sensitive Offer", countdown clocks, and similar are all marketing tactics to get you to purchase right away by creating urgency. It's a good tactic and it works! But being aware that these are simple techniques will help you in choosing a good product as opposed to one that sucks eggs.

Along with those urgency techniques, also understand that not everything presented on a "sales page" is what it seems on the surface. Take for instance testimonials. It's important for you to know how some businesses get these and why. First, let's discuss how they get them. A lot of times, authors of products will offer a free copy of their product in exchange for a testimonial. And who wouldn't love something they had to pay nothing for? In some cases, getting that free copy and providing a positive testimonial is a requirement and not a request. Still yet, other times, the author will ask for feedback to perform final "tweaks" on the product before the official release, and then as a follow-up, will ask those that participate for a nice little testimonial to which they offer the participants a "link back" to their own page. It's free publicity. And another darn good way to gain your trust and get you to believe more firmly in the product so that you purchase it.

Furthermore, the reason why those in the online business need these testimonials is to gain your trust in them and their product. Word of mouth carries a lot of weight when it comes to customers purchasing something from you. Again, another marketing tactic that works, and works well.

Always remember that everything you see isn't always so cut-and-dry. Some things are going on "behind the scenes" that you don't know about. Are these things dishonest? To a certain degree? But some offer completely genuine testimonials. Are there sales pages out there that speak the truth about the products they are selling? Sure. The unfortunate part is that it's very difficult to know the difference. And the reason for this is that some internet marketers know what they're doing.

Now, where can you get high-quality products for a good deal? One of the best places is through private membership websites. These types of sites are stocked with plenty of resale right information products to get you up and going. Plus, they almost always have several products that are up to date, or just released recently available for you to download.

Collecting your information products this way will most definitely save you money in the long run. Add to this the fact that there are products you can choose from and decide which you feel are worth selling to your customers.

Plus, when you resell these products, which most, if not all, come with resale rights, you stand to make 100% profits from them, excluding selling fees from companies such as PayPal, eBay, etc. I guarantee that having just one high-quality resource for your information products, as Allan's is, will bring you a much bigger return on your initial investment of having that membership on a monthly basis when you put your selling skills to work.

There is yet another way to get a decent amount of resalable information products for the cost of but one. You can purchase a "package" of them. Whether this is done by a special sale or a specific product, you will always get your money's worth if you spend your money in the right places.

With packaged information products, you must, again, be very selective. Many resellers the method I like to call "recycling". This is where they will take a bunch of older products and repackage them giving the overall effect of this package being something new. While in essence, it is something new, the outer package, what's inside is just the same old stuff.

The best way to avoid buying those information product titles you already have is to read the sales page and look for a list of products included within the package. Most will have this information up there, including an image. If it doesn't, skip it and move on to the next one. If all it has is a title, skip it. You need an honest description of the package so you can determine whether you have those exact products already so you're not "double buying".

And to help you out, I want to provide you with a few outstanding titles that won't cost you one red cent. Consider it a gift for purchasing this guide. This way, you'll know what to look for by having an example provided to you. There is one other additional way that can bring you in some outstanding profits. And that is writing up and creating your very own information product. It's not as difficult as it might sound. And everyone has a story inside them just itching to get out. Even you!

2. **Physical Products**

Of course, you can always sell physical products through the internet too. A great way to begin this is by looking around your own home for items that you want to get rid of and selling them using an auction site such as eBay.

Practically anything can sell and fetch a pretty good price on eBay. In fact, one person was able to sell nothing! I don't recommend you do that personally as there are plenty of rules you must follow and doing something like this could get you permanently banned from buying or selling on eBay. So just make sure that you have a product to offer.

Also, when selling a physical product on eBay, you'll want to be sure that your descriptions are accurate. If there's a defect with what you're selling, explain it. Put it out there. This won't necessarily hurt your chances of making a sale, but not adding important information like this can.

Remember too, that since you are selling a physical product, it will need to be shipped out to the individual who bid highest or "bought it now". So, you'll need to add those costs to the price. eBay allows for this, but don't go overboard. Only charge what is necessary to ship the product. Don't be greedy. It will bite you in the end! And having over-excessive shipping charges will sometimes make it harder for you to sell your product. Then you'll be stuck with not only the item you were trying to sell but also the fees to list it.

It's important to add here that any type of information, or digital product you have, that has the resale rights, of course, can be converted into a physical product by placing it on a CD. In fact, eBay encourages you to sell information products in this way.

Now, I'm not going to delve into all the specifics of how to do this as that's not my area of expertise. And really, it goes beyond the scope of this guide. But I will provide you with some outstanding informative products that will.

We have figured out where to sell our products from, and what we should be selling. So now we need to understand who we should be selling these products to.

CHAPTER THREE

Who to Sell Your Products to

Knowing who you are selling specific products to is just as important, if not more so, than what you are selling them. How exactly can one find out just who their specific customers are? That's simple. Think about the item you are selling. What is it? Who would be most likely to purchase it? Who would benefit from it? These types of questions can narrow down your core selling base. And it will help you understand how to advertise your product and get a better response. Understanding your product completely will help you be more successful in the selling process, especially when potential customers have questions that you will need to be able to answer for them.

So, now that you know who you should be selling to, where do you go about finding this select group of individuals? Not too difficult. First off, high traffic sites like eBay for instance, are already comprised of hungry buyers. All they need do is put in a few keywords to search for what they want. There is a nice list provided for them. But be sure that you use as many descriptive words, or keywords, as you can when choosing a listing title for your product.

Say, if you are selling a DVD movie about Dracula. Then you might want to select something like this: Classic Dracula Horror DVD. You get the idea here. People searching for not only a DVD movie, but those searching for the keywords: horror, classic, and Dracula, will also see your listing. Always remember to be honest when you list any product anywhere for sale.

Another great way to find customers that are willing to receive notifications from you about certain products you are selling is by starting up your very own mailing list or newsletter. It's easy to start one and doesn't take too much time to operate. If you decide just to send previous customers special notices when you have new inventory, that's fine. But be sure that these people want to receive these mailings from you. Otherwise, you're spamming them. They have to agree to this type of action. It doesn't matter if they bought something from you. All they agreed to receive at the time of their purchase was the product they paid for. Nothing more. However, if you approach them in a friendly manner and ask them if they would like to receive future notices about your new products, many times they will agree to that if they are satisfied with your performance.

There are other ways to create your mailing list though. You can create a signup form on your website, use a popup or pop-under from your website, use free Joint Ventures, or offer free products to those that subscribe.

The bottom line is that previous customers can become repeat customers. And that's what you want! One last way I'd like to talk about is by getting traffic to your online store or website. Even if you decide to run a free site, you can still sell products there through the use of banner advertisements, or ad boxes such as those provided by companies like Google. While you may not generate "instant profits" by using this method, you can begin to make a steady trickle of money over time.

We're almost to the home stretch! All we need to do now is focus on how you can begin selling.

CHAPTER FOUR

How to Sell Your Products

There are plenty of creative ways that you can start marketing your products to potential customers. Of course, these aren't all the processes of profit generation, but those listed are some pretty darn good ones. Take some time to read up on each one and try them out. Everyone's path to success is a different one, and yours will be no exception. Most of the methods listed below are more commonly used for selling information products online but can be adapted to selling physical products also.

Keep in mind, these methods I've outlined for you below are just basic descriptions and there are many different products available that describe each one or a combination of them in lots more detail. Think of this as your "selling dictionary" so that when you begin learning the actual process of selling, you'll know many of the terms that are discussed ahead of time.

The Traffic Method

Using traffic exchange sites is a great way to begin sending floods of visitors to your online store or website. If people don't know about your business, then how do you expect to make any money from it? That's where these exchanges come in. Although, it's not without plenty of effort and time that will get those visitors to your site. If you want to participate for free, then expect to spend lots of time looking at other participants' websites to earn credits that go towards getting visitors to your site.

An alternative is to pay for traffic if this is within your budget. Understand though that just because you pay to get the people visiting your site doesn't mean that they buy, or even stay longer than 30 seconds. I would suggest that you try the free traffic generation options available to test the waters. There have been many informative eBooks written on the subject with new ones cropping up all the time due to the popularity of this method.

The Forum Method

This is a simple, but effective method. Forums have long been an incredible source of information. So why not start participating in them?! Use a basic search engine and find the right forum that discusses the subject matter that pertains to the products you are intending to sell. Join the forum. Read the posts. Offer your unique perspective on them. Be helpful. Be friendly.

Everything isn't always about selling, even though this is your main goal. There are plenty of routes to get you where you're headed. It's often said that you must give before you can receive. No truer words were ever spoken. Especially when selling online!

You must be prepared to give something away, even if it's just your own experience, friendly advice, or much-needed help by those also participating and accessing the forum. Remember also that there is an existing advertising space already available inside almost every single forum. The signature. This is where you want to place a link to your product, website, or service with a tiny bit of "mouthwatering" descriptive text. Use that space! It's just as important as participating in the forums. You want to get the word out, so do so in a rather unobtrusive way with the signature tag.

The Blogging Method

Starting your own blog is not only easy, but it can also be very therapeutic. And in some cases, very lucrative! Many bloggers are making nice profits just from their blogs alone. How can you do this? Simple! Set up a product review section that describes your personal opinions on those products listed, and if you like them, be sure to add an affiliate link to them.

Or you could place banner advertisements on your blog and even charge others for placing their advertisement banners inside your blog. Also, you can add Google box ads inside your blog along the side or even within your posts. You could even have people interested in the information you provide inside your blog pay a monthly fee to access it. There are plenty of creative ways to profit from your blog.

The Affiliate Method

By far, this is the most inexpensive and easiest method to use. Every single day people just like you begin earning money from simply signing up for various affiliate programs. It won't cost you a thing past a few minutes to begin earning. That is, you need to become an affiliate before you can see any rewards. Most affiliate programs will give you all the information and tools you need to begin seeing profits. They want you to succeed. Otherwise, if you fail, they do too, and no money is made for either end. A word of caution though, not all affiliate programs are created equal. Or even close! Some pay their affiliates and some, well, beat around the bush and it could take up to 3-6 months to see even one dime from them. Be sure that you read all information available on any affiliate program beforehand. Time is an extremely valuable commodity when doing business online, and you can't afford to waste it on products or programmes that bring you no results.

The Auction Method

Another popular method for newbies and experienced sellers alike. Explosive sites like eBay have millions of visitors per day, so it's easy to see why this is such a popular choice for selling products online. It can be incredibly easy to list an item for sale and make quick cash when needed with the use of online auctions. However, you must choose your prices, products, and descriptions very carefully to make good profits. This takes time of course to learn the best ways, but it can be well worth it so long as your earnings stay in the "black", or positive numbers.

To sell through an auction site all you need is an account through the site itself, which is normally free, a product, and a payment processor such as PayPal to get your money as fast as possible. And most big auction sites like eBay offer plenty of useful information along with step-by-step instructions to get you up and "auctioning" quick as a flash.

The "Upsell" Method

Upselling is a tactic in where you offer a product to your customers, they purchase it, and then they are given the choice on whether they would like to upgrade their purchase with another product. There are different variations of the upsell and its purpose is like that of the back-end method. Take for instance a product that comes in three different versions, a lite version usually something that is free but with limitations put on functionality), a standard version (most commonly with most features enabled within the product but less "comfort creatures" such as 24-hour support, upgrades, etc.), and a pro version (normally this one will have all the "bells and whistles like free lifetime upgrades to the product, a special license to profit from reselling the product, either a resale rights license or an exclusive affiliate program).

Using the lite version of the product, you can give it away as a gift and then those people you give it to will have the chance to upgrade the product to a less restrictive version. This is upselling in a nutshell. There are plenty of products created out there that use this method to earn more profits.

The Back-End Method

This method is very popular in the eBook information industry. What it does is give you the power to pull in more profits after you have made the initial sale to your customers by providing you with specific links enabling the reader of the product to buy other related products. Thus, creating a built-in back-end sales force that runs on autopilot.

Imagine, if you will, having a product that you can not only resell repeatedly but one that has additional purchase links to other associated products within it bringing in more profits to you without you having to do nothing more than distributing the original file.

It's a very easy way to earn extra money after the first sale when you have a good product with a strong back-end. Changing these back-end links to point to your own special affiliate links is also referred to as "rebranding". However, full rebranding gives you special permission and tools to change other important details that help drive traffic to your site by providing you with other rebrandible links and text you can change letting your customers know who has provided this rich resource of information to them, and most importantly, where they can get more!

The "FireSale" Method

I'm sure you have seen this or at least heard of it before. This is when a company or organization has a massive sale at an extremely discounted price to move their merchandise.

Firesales have gained in popularity because of the sheer amount of profits being pulled in from them. It's not unreal to hear people say that they earned thousands of dollars in just 3 days. That's the power of the Firesale. A good Firesale will offer top quality products for an insanely low price, with the price going up by any given percentage or dollar amount throughout the length of the sale. It builds like a fire! Until it's all over and it has burned out or run its course.

There are some marketers that sell products online who dismiss these types of sales and never get involved in them. I feel they are doing themselves a great disservice this way. If you can get some great products for an unheard-of price, why not? There are specific tools you need to run such a sale and speaking from experience I have to say that John Delavera has one of the best called JV Manager. It's pricy but worth every single penny. Of course, there are others, but my money is on John all the way.

In addition, you'll need to have your own domain and webspace that allows you to upload and access .cgi and, or .php files since many of these types of Firesale programs run on this scripting.

The Membership Method

Creating your own membership site is a very profitable business. It also creates a stable flow of monthly income on a regular basis. That's what makes this method a great one.

Consider this, you could utilize a content management system such as PostNuke or Mambo and run the whole thing just from it. If you're more inclined to offer a place that is specifically for downloading products like those of the information or eBook nature, then a file hosting system like TradeBit may be the way for you to go. Or you could even run a membership website from your very own webspace with a script such as Membership Millionaire.

It's not a very difficult method to use, but it is quite time-consuming. And there is a lot of stiff competition with this type of site because it is such a successful method. So, you must think of a way to put a unique spin on whatever it is you are offering. For instance, you could give your members original content, private forums to build a helpful community, video tutorials, etc. This will bump up the value of your membership site over that of your competition. Usually, this method doesn't do that well on auction sites since many of those searching through there are looking for the lowest price they can find.

The "Recycle" Method

Recycling old products for profit is not a new idea. People have been doing this with paper, cans, and other assorted items for years. When you are offering an unused or used product in your possession for sale, you are recycling it. So, it is with information products too. But there's a difference here.

When you offer a used physical product for sale, you offer it one time, get paid one time, and that's all there is to it. When you sell a resalable information product, you can sell it as many times as you can, and can profit with back-end affiliate links or add a free sign-up form for your mailing list, generating new leads and more profits over and over again. Now, when an information reseller has products that are a bit older, they will take these and package them up.

In other words, they recycle them and can take something that's been on the market for a while, give it a "facelift" with new graphics and new sales copy. They have an all-new profit generation system. However, they do need to add a few new things within the collection of the recycled products. It makes it much easier to get buyers this way. In my book, Info Product Recycling, this process is clearly explained with more in-depth information on adding this method to your selling arsenal.

The Viral Method

Ever heard the saying, "You don't get something for nothing."? Well, this method power-blasts that into dust! Just what is a "viral" product? Think of it as a nasty bug. And this little bug carries itself everywhere until it creates a full-blown virus. That's what this method is all about.

You create your own unique product on whatever topic you decide on, add lots of good information and affiliate links inside it, and then give it away. Yes. I said give it away. Everyone likes getting something for free. What makes this method even better than just giving great information away is the fact that you create a product that is chock full of back-end affiliate links for those that receive it from you to change those back-end links so they can profit by giving it away.

So how are you supposed to profit after the downloaders have changed all those links? That's easy! By adding your own advertisements that cannot be changed with your affiliate or direct purchase links throughout! You could put one or two on every single page or before every chapter of your informative product. Even though all the other back-end affiliate links can be changed, those ads cannot. So, you'll still generate profits or mailing list sign-ups even though you're giving this specific product away.

Things to Avoid

When starting up any business, there are certain pitfalls you need to steer clear of. That's what this section is all about. So that you can arm yourself with the knowledge of techniques that will lead you down the path to failure. Whether that is time or money losses. Both are important!

I must add here that these things to avoid are things that I have tried myself and haven't brought me any positive results from using them. You should be cautious before you attempt any of these listed here.

Email Address Buying

I'm sure that you've seen these companies before. Some work, some don't. Most of them don't. And, unless you can be sure that these email addresses they are giving you are truly double opt-in (this is the process of saying "Sure! Send me information" digitally through a doubled process to be certain that those individuals do want the information that's being sent to their email addresses), and not harvested emails (emails that are randomly collected from around the internet with no idea they are being put on lists), it's like taking a shot in the dark.

Anyone can tell a lie. But it takes a great person to tell the truth. Sad to say, there's not a whole lot of those kinds of people doing business on the internet. But there are still some folks out there you can trust by building a long relationship with them.

I'll tell you this much, the best way to build your mailing list is to do this on your own. This way, you are 100% sure that the email addresses you have and the people behind them really want what you are sending out to them. I would recommend that you think twice, and then think again before purchasing any email addresses from anyone. Especially if the price is low.

Safelist Mailing

In a word, NO! Safelists comprised others trying to sell their products to each other. It doesn't work. Most of the time, if not all the time, your email ad will go unnoticed and be deleted on site. Sure, safelists can be joined for free, but remember, you get what you pay for.

So, if you're paying nothing, expect the same in return. I have personally paid for safelist memberships and have seen an absolute lack of profit return from mailing to them. And the same is true for free safelists. It's a process that's been around for a while, but it simply doesn't work, and you'd do well to invest your time in a worthy joint venture giveaway instead. At least you'd get something out of it!

SPAMMING

This one is simple and can be summed up with just one sentence. SPAM is against the law in the U.S. If you're caught doing it, and you will most likely get caught, you will be fined and could have your computer equipment confiscated. There's no reason to SPAM people. It's annoying and doesn't do a thing for you except ruining your reputation.

Time Wasters

These are a collection of "get rich quick schemes". They are lurking in every corner of the internet. Don't participate in them. Money rotator programs don't work. Pyramid schemes don't work. And the list could go on and on. These are serious time wasters and will not make you rich. They're crap. Plain and simple. The only real people benefiting from these types of programs are the ones who created the darn things! Think about it. You find this program that sounds pretty good. It only costs you a total of $5.00 to get in. Your member's name is put on a list and randomly displayed to get paid for every new member that signs up. But you only make $2.00. The program creator/operator makes the other $3.00.

And they get paid every single time a new member signs up. You however are put in a pot of countless thousands whose member names get randomly rotated. The owner is sure to get paid, you aren't. Plus, you have to get out there and start recruiting others not even sure that you'll get paid by doing so. See what I'm saying here? It's only quick money for those running the program. Not you.

The "Failure" Factor

This is one of the greatest success crushers there is. And it's all caused by negative thinking and giving up! If you don't have a big following of personal supporters like family and friends, don't worry about it! You won't get anywhere positive if you let the negative comments inside your head. You've got to put those things on the back burner to be successful at selling products online. To heck with the nay-sayers. Are they feeding your family? Are they paying your bills? No. YOU ARE!

Every single person has the mental capacity within themselves to be a success at anything they do in life. That includes you. So, what if Aunt Sally thinks you're nuts for trying to make money online. Who cares if your brother or sister can't get a grasp on what you're trying to accomplish?

What matters is what your goals are and what you believe you can do.

A wonderful saying to remember is: "If you can believe it, you can achieve it!" You can do this. It's not brain surgery. And if your first idea is a total flop, so what? Get back on that horse and try again. This is where many give up. Not everything you do will be the best course of action. But you will gain the necessary experience through failure so that you can succeed the next time. But you must give "next time" a chance. Remember, "If at first you don't succeed, try and try again". If you give yourself enough time to learn and grow your internal knowledge base, you will succeed.

"Too Good to Be True" Products or Sellers

And finally, always remember, if it seems too good to be true, it probably is. Now, not everything will be a "too good to be true" product or service. There are some people and companies out there that have terrific services and products at unbeatable prices. Never judge a book by its cover. Read all the details. Make certain you understand everything in a merchant's terms. If you don't, ASK QUESTIONS! Any reliable merchant should be able, and willing, to answer them. If you do ask, and don't hear one single word back, or it takes them an unexplainable amount of time to provide you with the answers you seek, pass that offer over and move on to the next one.

In conclusion, selling products online can be an exciting and profitable business. But you have to be very careful with everything you do. Every transaction you make. Every friendship you strike up. Use your common sense. It will carry you far in your quest for internet riches.

Facebook and Your Business

You've been working very hard to introduce your business to as many potential targeted customers as possible – the ones who will find your products irresistible, and eagerly spend money. You've done it through SEO, social networking, press releases, article marketing and perhaps even a pay-per-click campaign like Google AdWords. In short, you've used all the traditional (and not so traditional) ways that help online businesses catch on like wildfire.

But have you considered marketing on Facebook yet? If not, you may not be aware of this comparatively new source of targeted customers – the sort who you may not be able to reach by traditional means. Facebook is one of those phenomena online that the smart marketer can't ignore. It's the Internet's largest social network site with hundreds of millions of active users.

There are many ways to market on Facebook. Some ways are free, and some would cost you money. You will discover how you can get floods laser targeted traffic and build your brand and name easily to increase your profits. If you are not using this lucrative way to market your business, you are leaving wads of cash lying on the table. Read on to find out how you can benefit from Facebook in your online business.

Why Use Facebook to Market Your Business?

Facebook is currently the biggest social media and networking platform on the planet. Marketing is a numbers game and if you are not tapping into a market as big as this, your competition will leave you in the dust! Facebook is becoming so big that it overtook Google as the website that got the most traffic in a single day. This means that Facebook is becoming bigger than Google itself. How would you like a piece of that pie?

Facebook is also a great place to "soft sell" your products because a lot of normal users don't know that you can use Facebook as a marketing platform for your business. Not only that but there is also a way to generate targeted visitors that some people don't even know about. Those of them that don't know this is losing out big time. Do you want to be one of those people or do you want to leave your competition cleaning up behind you for a few scraps?

Another great reason for marketing with Facebook is that there are so many ways to use this website to market your websites and products and many ways to turn these users into cash. You can use profile updates, friends' requests, groups, fan pages, events, social ads, the marketplace, pictures, videos, and a lot more. You will find out exactly how you can use all these free techniques to generate massive amounts of targeted website visitors easily, as well as learn how to use the social media ads of Facebook to get those targeted visitors to your sites and page. These ads are probably the most targeted form of traffic on the internet today.

What Is Facebook Advertising?

You've seen them yourself, most likely... those ads running down the right-hand side of your Facebook pages, most of them about interests you particularly enjoy. You are not seeing the same ads as everyone else accessing Facebook at that moment. These are specifically targeted to data Facebook has gleaned from your preferences and other sources.

Facebook ads are simple but powerful. Each one consists of a title, text block and graphic or photo of your choice – all within a 110px X 80px "box", to fit that vertical, right-hand Facebook sidebar. If you think of them as a cross between a Twitter tweet and a banner ad, you've just about got the picture!

And yes – they absolutely can advertise your:

- Product
- Services
- Contest
- Cause
- Links
- Photos
- Videos
- Business USP
- Business Event

As well as integrating:

- Your offline promotions with your online
- Real-time information for your consumers

Facebook Advertising Benefits

SEO vs. Social Trends – Facebook's biggest benefit is most obvious. It operates through social networking and trending rather than pure SEO – the hottest trend of this brand-new decade. It allows readers to see your ads on their mobile phones – and mobile devices now outnumber personal computers, 4 to 1!

It is also cheaper than Google AdWords, and while the latter is still a wonderful way to kick-start a campaign, AdWords can be risky for newer marketers, as costs per click can skyrocket faster than your sales. Will it replace AdWords completely? That shouldn't be your goal! Plan further down the line to do what the big boys and girls do: Kick-start each campaign with well-optimized and researched AdWords.

Facebook vs. AdWords Costs: But whether you use AdWords (SEO based) or Facebook ads (social networking based), Facebook ads nowadays are a "must" – particularly with the not-so-subtle switch over to mobile devices! But it's great for beginning marketers because now, it's significantly less expensive to advertise on Facebook than with PPC!

Graphics Capability: Its other biggest benefit is that you can introduce a graphic element or photo into what is just a small text ad! Since Facebook is "tuned" to graphic elements, and interest has been shown to peak when graphics are displayed, it wins hands-down over AdWords tired, irritating banner ads (traditionally low converters for over a decade). You could simplify it like this: Want a text ad only? – Use AdWords. Plan to use a graphic? – Use Facebook Ads.

Text Capability: You have 75 words to say what you want to say in Google AdWords (that's less than half a tweet!) Facebook ads not only allows you a 25-character headline but 135 words of body text, too. (That's over double Google AdWords' capacity – but note; spaces count.)

Does SEO Still Apply?

It is crucial to the success of your Facebook Ad! Remember when we talked about Facebook Ads geared to your specific hobbies, tastes, preferences, and interests appearing down the right-hand side of your Facebook page? You'll notice that:

- Some don't appeal to you
- A small percentage make you click on them right away
- ... and yet a third group appeals to you, but it may take you <u>days of repeated exposure</u>, seeing the same ad <u>many times</u>, before you finally give up and click through.

You want your ad to be in the latter 2 categories. And you achieve that through solid, well-researched long-tailed keywords (combined with your irresistible, curiosity-arousing 25-character headline and 135 character body text).

Get those elements right, and you'll have an ad that bypasses casual searchers (how many right-hand-side Google search page paid ads do you ever click on, compared to Facebook Ads?) and zeros in on a 75% pre-sold, pre-qualified market.

Who Is It For?

Some people will tell you that Facebook Ads don't work for business purposes, but that's simply not so. It should speak volumes and give you a big, fat clue about its potential when you realize that major companies are taking full advantage of Facebook Ads, in creative ways. For example, according to Facebook's own Marketing Solutions page:

- **Honda** recently used Facebook Ads to keep consumers updated (and do serious damage control) after its recent spate of shocking recalls.
- **Budweiser** encouraged social interactivity with its customers when it invited them to select which commercials to show during televised sports games.
- **Guitar Hero** became the first online video game to reach 1,000,000 fans on Facebook

Even **Coca-Cola** jumped on the bandwagon, selling "virtual bottles of coke" and promising to donate $1.00 for every virtual bottle sent to their favourite cause.

These 4 examples alone show you the sort of <u>creativity</u> you can employ (and <u>flexibility</u> you can take advantage of) when creating your Facebook Advertising campaign!

"Fansumers"

If you've been wondering what a "fansumer" is, it's yet another social phenomenon you can use to your advantage.

According to Forrester Research, a "fansumer" is simply a consumer who has "become a fan" of a brand on Facebook.

This brings us back to Facebook Ads' third biggest advantage … interactivity.

It's a proven maxim: Get people to engage as a participant, rather than as a spectator, and their stake in what they're engaging in becomes <u>personal </u>and more <u>positive</u>. Use an app or a product and click the little "become a fan" text link on your Facebook page, and you are not only contributing to its statistical popularity but <u>personally endorsing</u> it!

This can help 2 particular types of "product" in particular...

1. **Apps** (applications such as Zynga's "Farmville" game)
2. **Brands**

Allowing people to become Facebook fans should be a definite part of your branding campaign... and as for Farmville's meteoric rise, it is legendary. One only has to take a glimpse at its U.S. Alexa rank of 370 to see how powerful this can be.

Alexa summarizes this popular app game thus: "... farmville.com is visited more frequently by **females** who are in the age range**18-24**, received **some college** education and browse this site from **home**."

This is right in line with Facebook's "18-34 female" broad demographic – but the truth is, you can certainly reach other target customers in different demographics if you take a close look at Farmville's stats from Quantcast.com:

Keeping in mind that a less broad and **<u>more specific</u>** demographic is likely to be yours (unless you create a truly buzzworthy product like Farmville) you can certainly play to small niche Facebook markets.

A good rule of thumb is to make sure the niche customer you wish to reach does operate via social networking at least as much as – if not more than – through standard PC use and Google searches. You can also target specific geographic areas, using Facebook Ads (by country, state or province, town, or city). And remember, when someone brands him or herself as your fan (or "fansumer"), they are letting you know they are ripe for your offerings.

Why Profile Pages are Your Friends!

The main reason you can target so specifically, despite Facebook itself having a broad, generic demographic, can be attributed to profile pages.

Think about it: When you filled out your profile page, you were prompted to share your:

- Hobbies and interests
- Career and work information
- School, college, or university
- Tastes in music, books, and movies
- Personal and contact information (date of birth, marital status, etc.)
- City and state

And as much extra information as you chose to share.

Among the things you share you can bet people can find great long-tailed keywords! These are what you should use when creating your Facebook Ads – targeted specifically to your ideal customer, of course. Use your keyword in your headline at the very least – and again in the text (provided it feels natural: Remember, Facebook puts "social" before "SEO").

The Mechanics of Facebook Ads

In addition to the creative side of your Facebook Ads, there are other actions you can choose to take. You can:

- Pay per click (PPC)... or per impression (CPM)
- Track your Ad's progress in "real-time"
- Edit and tweak your ads, for your best results

Best of all, Facebook Ads are easy to set up, with a step-by-step process that guides you clearly through the creation and all your options.

Facebook is quietly becoming the newest 2010 trend in online advertising – especially for those on a budget – as of this writing. Even if you don't think it's right for your business, you are to be applauded for taking the time to at least learn more about it!

Free ways to market on Facebook.

While Facebook ads could be one of the most targeted and profitable ways to market on Facebook, you can also use Facebook in a lot of other ways to market your products and websites. The starting point for your presence on Facebook is your profile page. Your profile page is basically a landing page that you design to convert your friends to engage with certain parts of your identity.

If you want to use this free marketing strategy, the secret is to expand your network as much as possible. The way to do this is to expand! Start a group and you create a central place for customers, partners, and friends to participate in conversations around your brand. Facebook groups come with boards for posting discussion topics, photos, videos, and links right out of the box. And the best part about Groups is you can create as many as you like for free.

While Groups do offer a reasonably robust feature set with no setup, you're not able to extend their functionality with Facebook applications. In order to use those, you will need to get a Facebook Page.

Pages were launched by Facebook in November 2007 as a way for businesses of many types to easily establish a brand presence on Facebook. Pages are more customizable than groups. You can add HTML, Flash, or even Facebook applications to your pages to extend their functionality. Pages are a good option for small or local businesses that want to establish a presence on Facebook. Like groups, they're another free and easy way to do viral marketing.

You can also join a network marketing group, send out several comments, write notes, add friends, add events, join events, wall post on Groups, wall post on Friends Walls, post videos in Groups, cross-pollinate with other Group Owners, add many photos, make sure all your privacy settings are OFF. Never forget that Facebook is a society so don't try to be a seller, try to solve others' problems. Community is about communication, and that might be the best advertising you could hope for.

'Brands' are already networking and engaging with consumers via Facebook for leverage, strengthening and generating a better understanding of the brand itself and customer relationships with it, and for participation and valuable feedback. Don't underestimate the power of this free tool, you can connect with people around the world so easily.

Tips To Get Viral Traffic with Facebook

By using Facebook effectively, you can easily start getting traffic virally if you know how to leverage this source of traffic. Here are 7 Tips to Getting Traffic with Facebook Viral Marketing.

1. Get More Friends

Friends are the most important aspect of social networking as they are needed to make money! The more friends you have, the more visibility your business will have, which ultimately leads to more sales for you.

2. Get a Blog

Blogs are a great way to spread the word about your business. You can incorporate your blog into your Facebook account and add RSS feeds for your readers to follow up on. You can also comment on other blogs linking back to your site.

3. Use Your Picture Wherever You Can

Uploading your picture can get you a lot more views of your articles/comments than those without pictures. Spammers never take the time to upload a picture. Also, people like having a face with a name and it makes them trust you a lot more.

4. Have a Great Profile Page

If you are a big social networker, you will have a pimped-out profile page. Link to all your social network profiles and personal projects to gain maximum exposure. Promote your RSS feed from your blog on your profile page. Make it attractive with enough information so it doesn't look boring!

5. Use the Notes and Events Features

Sending notes and events are great ways at gaining more exposure in your business. If your friends like it, they may even pass them on to their friends. It's a win-win for everyone!

6. Create Good Content

Content is king. If you are a good writer in a popular niche, then you will have no problem succeeding in social networking sites like Facebook. People like great content and they will take the time to read it if it piques their interest. Try to write articles that include lists, like "Top 10..." or "7 Reasons Why...".

7. Give Away Free Stuff

Everyone loves free stuff and your social networking friends will love you for it! Give them a free ebook, or maybe an article you found online. It doesn't have to be big. Anything that is helpful and related to your niche will be greatly appreciated by your friends.

These are just 7 of the many ways that you can capitalize on the social networking craze. These sites aren't going anywhere and are only going to grow. Start marketing now so you can be ahead of the 90% of other marketers out there!

www.ingramcontent.com/pod-product-compliance
Lightning Source LLC
Chambersburg PA
CBHW031004180726
47993CB00018B/1565